A Guide for a Successful Relationship: Better Together

by Demetra Jones Lewis

EDITED BY JHORDYNN (318) 406-2249

COVER PICTURE TAKEN BY WOODROW M. EVANS

COVER DESIGNED BY MARTINIS L. STEPHENS

COVER FORMATTED BY PSALMYY ON FIVERR

PUBLISHED BY MADE 4 THIS™

COPYRIGHT © 2021. ALL RIGHTS RESERVED

Paperback ISBN: 978-1-7348574-8-1

No part of this book can be replicated or duplicated without reference to the book. No part of this book may be stored in a retrieval system, database, and/or published in any form or by any means, electronic, mechanical, photocopying, recording, or otherwise, without the prior written permission of the author.

Thank you for reading. May this book be a blessing to your relationship.

Better Together is a class for couples that I host every first Tuesday of the month from 6-7 p.m. If you are in the area, please stop by and join us. We are located at Greater Blessing Church, 409 Sibley Road, Minden, LA 71055. The Under Shepherd is Superintendent/ Pastor Alvin Lewis. And I, Missionary Lady Demetra Lewis, am the instructor.

MISSION STATEMENT

To create a better, loving relationship between married couples so that their homelife will reflect Godly order and discipline that they may live with righteous integrity, to be a pattern for their children and communities through unity and having a Christ centered life, that God be glorified, and souls are won for His kingdom.

~I dedicate this book to my parents, the late Ralph and JoAlean Jones. They were married for 51 years before God called my mother home in August 2007. My parents taught me that no matter how many disagreements one may have, forgive and move on. They also instilled in me that family is important. They loved each other in their own special way. I thank them for being an example of "till death do us part". I vowed that I would do the same.~

Table of Contents

1. It's not Good for man to be Alone **(PAGE 1)**

2. Where two or Three are Gathered Together in my Name, There am I in the Midst of Them **(PAGE 5)**

3. What Does God say About the Duties of Man? **(PAGE 7)**

4. What Does God say About the Duties of Woman? **(PAGE 12)**

5. Why did you get Married? **(PAGE 15)**

6. Causes of Breakdown in Marriages. **(PAGE 18)**

7. How can we Fix It? **(PAGE 23)**

THANK YOU (PAGE 29)

1.

IT'S NOT GOOD FOR MAN TO BE ALONE

Gen. 1:26-27 (NIV) Then God said, "Let us make mankind in our image, in our likeness, so that they may rule over the fish in the sea and the birds in the sky, over the livestock and all the wild animals, and over all the creatures that move along the ground." So God created mankind in his own image, in the image of God he created them. Male and female he created them.

In Genesis 2:18 (NIV), The Lord God said, "It is not good for the man to be alone. I will make a helper suitable for him."

Genesis 2:18 (KJV) And the Lord God said, It is not good that man should be alone; I will make him an help meet for him.

Why? **Because we need each other.**

Genesis 2:22 (NIV) Then the LORD God made a woman from the rib he had taken out of the man, and he brought her to the man.

God didn't create woman from man's feet; she's not to be trampled on by man. God didn't create woman from man's head; she's not to rule over man. But God created woman from man's side—to be his help, assistance, extra hands. Man and woman are to conquer situations together at each other's side with God.

When God took the rib from Adam to create woman, she complemented him. God made her special, and she was to be treated as such. They were to live in harmony, not only with each other, but also with God. They were also to replenish the earth.

Proverbs 18:22 KJV- Whoso findeth a wife findeth a good thing, and obtaineth favour of the Lord.

Matthew 19:5-6 And he said, "'This explains why a man leaves his father and mother and is joined to his wife, and the two are united into one.' Since they are no longer two but one, let no one split apart what God has joined together." Husband and wife must form a relationship with one another without outside interferences.

Mark 10:2-9 (NKJV) The pharisees came and asked Him, "Is it lawful for a man to divorce his wife?" testing Him. And He answered and said to them, "What did Moses command you?" They said "Moses permitted a man to write a certificate of divorce, and to dismiss her." And Jesus answered and said to them, "Because of the hardness of your heart he wrote you this precept. But from the beginning of the creation, God 'made them male and female.' 'For this reason a man shall leave his father and mother and be joined to his wife, and the two shall become one flesh'; so then they are no longer two, but one flesh. Therefore what God has joined together, let not man separate."

BETTER TOGETHER.

Jot down any/ all of your thoughts and feelings related to this chapter.

_____

_____

_____

_____

_____

_____

_____

2.

WHERE TWO OR THREE ARE GATHERED TOGETHER IN MY NAME, THERE AM I IN THE MIDST OF THEM.

Since you married, is God in the midst?
_____

Deuteronomy 32:30 (KJV) "How should one chase a thousand, and two put ten thousand to flight, except their Rock had sold them, and the Lord had shut them up?"

One can chase one thousand, but two in unity (agreement) can do much more! Couples should learn to pray together and more will get accomplished because **GOD IS IN THE MIDST!**

If God is not in your marriage, it will not work like it was designed to work (in unity).

We have different roles in a relationship, but we have to be unified and work as one in order for our homes to be blessed.

For example, if the woman cooks, the man can wash the dishes. If the woman works and the man stays at home, he can clean the house.

What is/ are your spouse's role(s) in your marriage?

_____
_____
_____
_____
_____

What can you do to help your spouse in order to work together as a unit?

_____
_____
_____
_____
_____
_____
_____
_____

3.

WHAT DOES GOD SAY ABOUT THE DUTIES OF MAN?

First for the man (husband), then for the woman (wife), this is the whole duty of man according to Ecclesiastes 12:13-14 KJV: "Let us hear the conclusion of the whole matter: Fear God, and keep his commandments: for this is the whole duty of man. For God shall bring every work into judgment, with every secret thing, whether it be good, or whether it be evil."

It is **both** of our duty to fear God and keep his commandments. But what are our individual roles as it pertains to the home?

MAN (HUSBAND)

1 Corinthians 11:3— Christ is supposed to be the Head in the husband's life. In your marriage, is the husband allowing Jesus to lead him? _____

If not, what will the husband do to allow Jesus to lead him?

Ephesians 5:25-32—The husband is supposed to love his wife as Jesus loved the church. Jesus loved the church so much that he *died* for her.

How deep is the husband's love for the wife in your marriage?

The wife is an extension of the husband. The husband is also supposed to love his wife as his own body. No mentally sane man wakes up and physically beats himself up. No mentally sane man starves himself outside of a fast. This means that no husband should abuse his wife in any shape, form, or fashion; he is to love and care for her in the way he loves and cares for his own body. He is also supposed to place his wife above his parents. Yes, he can still love and care for his parents, but his wife comes first.

In your marriage, does the husband love the wife as his own body?

_____

In your marriage, has the husband placed his parents where they are supposed to be—underneath the wife?

_____

If the answer is "no" to any of these questions, what Godly steps will be taken to correct it and be in God's order?

_____
_____
_____
_____
_____
_____
_____
_____
_____
_____
_____
_____
_____
_____

Titus 2:1-2— God's order is that the husband practices self-control, be careful in how he behaves, be worthy of respect, and sound in faith, in love, and in endurance.

Which of these areas does the husband need to improve on? How will he do these things?

_____
_____
_____
_____
_____
_____
_____

Jot down any/ all of your thoughts and feelings related to this chapter.

4.
What Does God say About the Duties of Woman?

Eph 5:33— Every wife **MUST** respect her husband. Respect is shown in the way that she carries herself, in the way that she talks to him, in the way that she looks at him, in her actions when he's not around. Respecting the husband also means that the wife doesn't allow or encourage others to disrespect her husband. Other people making fun of her husband should not be tolerated by the wife. The husband's friends making passes at the wife should not be allowed by the wife. The wife should respect, honor, and value her husband at **ALL** times.

In your marriage, does the wife respect the husband in all aspects?

_____

In what areas does the wife not respect the husband?

_____
_____
_____
_____
_____
_____
_____
_____

What will the wife do and/or change in order to respect her husband in every way?

_____
_____
_____
_____
_____
_____
_____
_____

Titus 2:3-5— The wife needs to be kind to everyone, and she should be sober minded. The wife is supposed to love her husband and children. It is also the duty of the wife to live wisely, work in their home, be submissive to her husband, and not bring shame on God's word.

What area does the wife need to improve on from a Titus 2:3-5 perspective? How will she do that?

_____
_____
_____
_____
_____
_____
_____

Jot down any/ all of your thoughts and feelings related to this chapter.

_____
_____
_____
_____
_____
_____
_____
_____
_____
_____

5.

WHY DID YOU GET MARRIED?

Why did you marry your spouse?

Was it love? (You just couldn't see yourself without him/her, and you knew that there was nothing you wouldn't do for him/her?)

Was it not wanting to be lonely? (You got tired of coming home to a quiet house every night, and there was no one to text during the day?)

Was it because you thought no one else wanted you? (No matter how you wore your hair or how good you smelled, no one approached you.)

Was it because it was out of duty? (The woman became pregnant, so getting married was just "the right thing to do".)

Was it because you both were burning? (Neither one of you could control your sexual desires, so you decided to marry rather than fornicate.)

Why did you get married?

_____

_____

_____

_____

_____

Whatever the case may be, you're married! And because you are married, you now have duties and responsibilities as a married person, according to God, that you must uphold.

BUILDING AND REBUILDING- God is still in the business of creating marriages. He desires to be the foundation stone of each union. Most marriages are based on nothing; it isn't surprising that many collapse. But it's never too late with God. At any point, if we turn over our lives and our marriages to him, he will become the foundation, the builder, and the rebuilder, if that's necessary, of that home. Even the broken pieces of our lives can be mended and repaired if we let God be God in every area of our human relationships.

-Jack Mayhall, "Marriage Takes More than Love" (NovPress)

Jot down any/ all of your thoughts and feelings related to this chapter.

_____

_____

_____

_____

_____

_____

_____

_____

_____

_____

_____

_____

_____

6.

CAUSES OF BREAKDOWN IN MARRIAGES

God is not the center. If you didn't have a Godly relationship when you were dating, there's a good chance that when you got married, you didn't invite God in. If you haven't allowed God into your marriage, you are not living by His principles that allow marriages to survive. If God is not the center of your marriage, it is not too late to allow Him in.

Lack of communication. A lot of times in marriages, especially after being married for over five years, the couple just stops having meaningful conversations with each other. Conversations become mundane and repetitive: "Pick the kids up from soccer practice at 6 tonight." "The light bill is due in three days." "Don't forget to pick up milk when you go to the store." Conversations about how your day went slowly fade away over time; therefore, your spouse doesn't know that you had a bad day at work. If your spouse doesn't know that, your spouse doesn't know to be more gentle in his/her approach when asking you why something wasn't done. In return, you lash out at your spouse for being an additional problem of the day when your spouse never knew there was a problem to begin with.

Selfishness. One of the spouses only thinks about him/herself. All the decisions that the spouse makes benefits only him/herself. The spouse never takes the other spouse's thoughts, feelings, or circumstances into consideration. Dealing with a selfish spouse can and will wear the other spouse out quickly. It is easy to feel unloved, uncared for, and unimportant when your spouse rarely considers you.

Mismanagement of money. A lot of sources state that financial issues is the number one cause of divorce. No, money isn't everything, but it's not *nothing*, either. Whether we like it or not, we need money to survive. We need money for food, shelter, clothing, transportation, adequate lighting—we even need money to be able to make more money. Being married to someone who repeatedly puts you in a financial bind makes it really hard to want to remain with that person. If your spouse frequently spends the mortgage money on a new wardrobe, you will find it difficult to want to remain married. If you don't have electricity on in your house because your spouse spent that money on concert tickets, you will find it challenging to continue to be married. When your spouse's mismanagement of money affects your livelihood and quality of life, marriage is the last thing you desire.

FALSE EXPECTIONS OF YOUR MATE. What you desire from your spouse and what your spouse desires from you need to be clear before marriage. If you have found yourself married with unclear expectations, it is now time to discuss them. Sometimes, our expectations of our mate aren't only false, but also unrealistic. It's not realistic for your spouse to work eight hours a day on his/her job, work eight hours a day on his/her own business, get the kids ready for school, pick them up from school, and have a steaming from scratch meal on the table seven days a week. If your spouse couldn't speak up for him/herself to other people when you were dating, your spouse can't speak up for him/herself now; expecting him/her to put his/her foot down with people is unrealistic.

SELFISH TRANSFORMATION

The real transforming work of marriage is the twenty-four-hours-a-day, seven-days-a-week commitment. This is the crucible that grinds and shapes us into the character of Jesus Christ... Marriage calls us to an entirely new and selfless life... Any situation that calls me to confront my selfishness has enormous spiritual value.
  -Gary Thomas, "Sacred Marriage" (Zondervan)

What has caused your marriage to breakdown?

Jot down any/ all of your thoughts and feelings related to this chapter.

_____

_____

_____

_____

_____

_____

_____

_____

_____

_____

_____

_____

_____

_____

_____

_____

7.

HOW CAN WE FIX IT?

The first step to fixing the problems in our marriages is admitting that there's a problem. Once you've admitted that there's a problem, the next step is to pray about the problem. Pray to God to help you fix the problems, pray to God to fix you, pray to God to help you let Him fix the problems *and* you. **IF** you are blameless and your spouse is the only one who needs to be fixed, pray with your spouse for God to intervene and change what needs to be changed. Pray to God to soften your spouse's heart and allow him/herself to be changed by God. If the both of you have areas that need to be changed, pray together for each other and with each other; also, pray for your own individual self.

After you pray, **DO!** Prayer without works is dead. After you pray for the solution to your marriage, do the solution. After you pray for God to help you allow Him to change you, allow Him to change you!

There are a lot of things that we can do to fix the problems in our marriages, and each marriage is unique in the solution(s). But the one thing that is a solution to **ALL** marriages is **FORGIVENESS.** Once you forgive, and your spouse does something else, **FORGIVE AGAIN.** After you forgive again, **FORGIVE AGAIN.**

Forgiveness is a 24/7/365 decision. It is also a continuing constant. You can't forgive your spouse at 5 p.m., then at 8 p.m. throw in his/ her face what he/ she did. 1 Corinthians 13:5 states that charity (love) keeps no record of being wronged. You shouldn't be able to recall all the times that your spouse has wronged you. If you truly forgave him/her, and if you truly love him/her, it's not easy to remember their offences towards you. Depending on the offence, of course, you won't forget it. But it shouldn't be at the forefront of your mind from the time that you wake up to the time that you go to bed.

Matthew 6:12—the model prayer—teaches us to ask God for forgiveness of our sins **AS WE FORGIVE** those who have sinned against us. We can't ask for what we aren't willing to give. If we want God's grace and mercy, we must have grace and mercy towards others, including our spouses. Luke 6:36 states, "You must be compassionate, just as your Father is compassionate."

We seem to have grace, mercy, compassion, and tenderness towards everyone, except our husbands and wives. It seems as though everyone can receive a gentle answer from us, except our husbands and wives. It seems as though we can forgive everyone in the world for doing the most foul things to us, but we can't forgive our husbands and wives for doing the most minute things. We have chosen to do life with our spouses. That's hard enough in itself. Let's not make it harder by holding on to things that could be resolved with an "I understand, and I forgive you."

Let's be honest. None of us have been the best towards our spouses all the time. We all have taken our spouses for granted and used them to our advantage at one point in time. We all have lied to our spouses at some degree. We all need forgiveness from our spouses in one way or another. The same way we want our spouses to forgive us, let us forgive them.

Matthew 18:21-22— Then Peter came to him and asked, "Lord, how often should I forgive someone who sins against me? Seven times?" "No, not seven times," Jesus replied, "but seventy times seven!" 490 times we are to forgive someone. But Jesus never said how often to forgive 490 times. 490 times an hour? 490 times a day? 490 times a lifetime? Even if we knew how often, who can keep count of 490 times? Let's just forgive each other. And forgive each other again. And when we say we are done forgiving and can't forgive anymore, let's forgive one more time.

If you still need a picture of what true forgiveness looks like, read the entire book of Hosea. Between Hosea's forgiveness towards his promiscuous wife and God's forgiveness towards idol worshippers, you will really understand what forgiveness is.

Forgiveness is how marriages recover. Forgiveness is how marriages are restored. Forgiveness is how marital problems are fixed. Forgiveness is the answer. Every time.

WE ARE BETTER TOGETHER.

Jot down any/ all of your thoughts and feelings related to this chapter/ book.

_____

_____

_____

_____

_____

_____

THANK YOU

Thank you, Lord for trusting me with this ministry. I pray that I am bringing glory to your name. Thank you for blessing me with a marriage that has survived every attack Satan has thrown our way.

To my husband Supt Alvin L. Lewis, thank you for loving me in spite of my many flaws. You are my one and only. There will be no other. I love you. Thirty -four years and counting. Until death separates us. We are better together.

I thank my children Ebony, Justin, and Chris, and my niece Shanfer for your love and support to this ministry. May God continue to bless your marriages. I love you.

Thank you to everyone who has purchased and/ or read this book. I pray it blesses your marriages. If you are not married, I pray this book has prepared you for marriage.

Lastly, I want to thank Jhordynn, the editor of this book, for your gift. May God bless you in all you do.

Please leave a review wherever reviews are accepted

www.ingramcontent.com/pod-product-compliance
Lightning Source LLC
Chambersburg PA
CBHW041817040426
42452CB00001B/4